Foreword

First, let me start by saying, parenting is the hardest role you will ever have in your life!

*I mean it...***no one is perfect at this task**, including me! If you are a parent, then you have had your fair share of struggles. If you are just becoming a Mom or Dad, congratulations and buckle up!!! You are in for a surprising and rewarding ride.

Each child is a unique gift to the world. Some kids are submissive and quiet, while others are stubborn and loud. Many youngsters figure out how to get on your very last nerve and wear you down into submission. I understand! Misbehavior and meltdowns can be very challenging for anyone.

Parenting is hard!

After teaching for over 30 years, however, I saw mothers and fathers using brilliant strategies to raise amazing citizens. I've noticed many consistent approaches being used by these successful parents. This book represents the best practices of what I have seen over that period and my own family experiences. Keep in mind these handy tips will not fit every child in all circumstances. However, having predictable routines and order in your life will help you navigate the world of raising children.

Believe it or not, toddlers, youth, and teenagers crave structure! It is a large part of what makes them feel loved and secure. Successful parents know kids require love, limits, time, and plenty of attention. It is your responsibility as a mother and/or father to create this stable world. Be the boss and protect your children from growing up too fast. The number one rule of raising a healthy family is: **Mothers and fathers need to be in charge at home!**

Appreciations

- I dedicate this book to all the Moms and Dads out there doing their best to raise joyful, healthy children.

- My sisters and I feel we had the finest parents in the world! My Mom, Reesie, did an amazing job raising four daughters. Many of these lessons came from her, and from the countless experiences I had throughout my teaching career! I can only hope my daughter feels the same way about me, as I do about my Mom. My daughter is my greatest accomplishment!

- I send forth appreciation and admiration to my teacher friends who helped me with their expert advice and insightful council for those 30-plus years.

- I would like to acknowledge Oprah and Dr. Phil for many decades of thought-provoking life lessons!

- One giant "thank you" goes out to Shauna for her beautiful illustrations! Your hard work and talent shine through on every page.

- My sister, Donna, was the most influential in helping this book come to light. She read it repeatedly and without complaint. I am so thankful to her and her expansive knowledge of the English Language. She provided many helpful suggestions to achieve this final copy of "Simple Steps to Parenting."

- Last, I gratefully give a shout out to Molly, Richie, my family, and my friends who encouraged me to follow my dreams...

A...Admiration

Children will be looking up to you as a role model. Strive to be the type of person your child will admire! Set the tone and be a positive example for them to follow. The wise old saying is true: **"Actions speak louder than words."**

Cursing and swearing around little ones is inappropriate. You should choose to use healthy vocabulary when you are around them. Show them your best self!

Express your admiration of them, too! Let them see it in your eyes as well as your words.

B...Behavior

Children are quite capable of appropriate behavior. Set expectations for them and reward their outstanding efforts. Conversely, giving in to unwanted actions will guarantee more poor choices. Take the time to teach your youngster, "You can't always get what you want."

Don't spoil your kids! They must learn to accept the word, "No." Let the meltdowns happen when they are young and in the privacy of your own home. Whining is a sign of being tired or trying to manipulate you. One of the best ways to respond to whining is to state, "Sorry, we can't do what you want right now because you are whining." The challenge: Don't give in or you will see these behaviors again!!!

C...Consequences

Children need consequences! **Kids will behave at their best when they know what we expect of them.** Little ones who misbehave should have a "*time-out*." A "*time-out*" does not mean they get to go to their room and play video games. A "*time-out*" *means* boredom and having nothing to do! Locate a quiet place for them to sit: the couch, a chair, or even the bottom of your steps (for a short amount of time!). After the "time-out" is over, be sure to tell your son or daughter you love them, you just didn't like their behavior. Use a calm voice to discuss what you hope to see in the future. Try to find out why they were acting out. Keep in mind a "*time-out*" works for parents, too! Occasionally, you need a minute to yourself just to maintain your own sanity!

As youngsters get older, losing a privilege may be the most appropriate course of action. Choose a length of time that makes sense. The time frame and consequence should be reasonable, so you will follow through. It is never okay to hit a child...ever!

D...Decisions

Parents should carry out important decisions for their children. Kids operate on what they want right now. Adults base their decisions on what's best for their families. **Speak with confidence and mean it!** Little ones will try to get their way by whining or crying. They prefer to be in charge! It is your job to keep that in check. Give them choices, "Would you like to play with your toys, read a story, or go to the park right now?" In this manner, you can lead them toward the activities you want them to pick. This also teaches youngsters how to make decisions for themselves.

Parenting is not happening if you allow your child to do whatever they choose. Don't let the tail wag the dog!

E...Electronics

Limit, Limit, Limit!!!

Put a strict limit on your child's electronic time.

Electronics are anything with a plug or a battery. Remember, this is going to be hard, not easy! Children will whine, beg, plead, and negotiate to get more minutes (even babies!). Think of all the other activities they are missing out on if you don't limit their E-Time. Reading is at the top of that list; using their imagination comes in a close second. **There is a time and place for youngsters to use electronics for entertainment.** Kids need to learn how to fix boredom on their own without electronics. It doesn't make your child any smarter to watch TV or play video games for hours. Anyone can swipe a screen sideways, even a one-year-old! Be leery of the electronic babysitter; it is lazy parenting!

Electronics...Part 2!

If you think taking electronics away from babies or toddlers is tricky, just wait until they are teens or preteens. Start by making a hard and fast rule from the beginning: **No electronics in your child's bedroom...period.** Studies have shown you will have smarter children if you remove any electronics from their rooms. Yes, this includes TV!

FYI: Teenagers will text each other throughout the night. Those late night texts will keep your son or daughter awake. The next day, your child will be exhausted and cranky. Just don't allow it from the start and save yourself from this aggravation. Sow the seeds of this early to avoid these pitfalls.

On that note, don't get lost in your own electronic bad habits!

F...Family

Keeping your family happy is the best gift you can give to your children. Sometimes it's a challenge to be kind and remain positive with one another. We all have fights. You should attempt to fight fair and guard your negative comments. Harsh words have staying power.

Build up your kid's confidence, so they feel empowered going out into the world.

Eat meals as a family every day and put your electronics away. They do not belong at the table while you are eating. Conversation is vital to learning new vocabulary and engaging in social interactions. Schedules get busy, but having dinner together teaches so many important life lessons. Don't underestimate its value!

G...Gratitude

Teach your children to be content with what they have right now. Kids who demand the newest toy or latest gadget will have trouble being satisfied. Take the time to highlight your blessings and remind them others may not be as fortunate.

Show your youngsters how to give back or pay it forward. Look for opportunities to volunteer in your community. Help a senior citizen rake, shovel, or do yard work. What a perfect way to demonstrate you care! Drop off cookies or a housewarming gift to a new neighbor. Imagine the self-esteem boost your child will get from completing this small gesture. Parents should perform random acts of kindness to set examples for young ones to follow.

H...Happiness

Happiness is a choice you and your child can make every day. You might be a Negative Nellie or a Gloomy Gus, but people would rather spend time with someone who is trying to stay upbeat. How will your children look at their world? Will they see it as half empty or near full of wonderful experiences? Help them notice the good in people and places around them.

Here's the thing: when you focus on finding the positive, you will attract more of the same. Conversely, I bet you can guess what happens if you are focusing on the negative. The choice is yours!

I...Imagination

Your youngster will only learn to use their imagination if they turn off their electronics. Everything that needs a plug or a charge should be shut down regularly! It is so sad to see children sitting side by side on their gadgets, not interacting with each other. Do something about it! Foster their creative minds by starting a box of recycled materials. Occasionally, add a few craft supplies like markers, colored paper, and glue sticks. They will love it! Encourage your youngsters to entertain themselves, invite a friend over, or create a project with their sibling.

Nudge your kids outside to play. Be the parent who pulls up a chair and watches their little ones interact in the neighborhood. Read a book, take pictures, or briefly check your emails to pass the time. Or take them to a local playground and introduce yourselves to some new friends.

J...Jobs/Chores

Boys and girls should contribute to the overall welfare of their home. Completing chores develops character and self-esteem. Having duties around the house creates the foundation for a strong work ethic. Jobs can be as simple as making their beds and cleaning their rooms to taking out the trash. Clearing the table, putting dishes into the dishwasher, vacuuming, and picking up toys are also tasks that kids can tackle at a fairly young age. These family assignments develop discipline and responsibility.

Earning a fee for chores can teach money skills like saving for long- and short-term goals. Have your son or daughter use three jars to manage their funds: today's wants, tomorrow's needs (college), and a donation jar.

K...Kick Back and Relax

Family life is so important to children. Youngsters love to spend time with their parents. It doesn't even have to be too complicated. Just go to the park, take them to the beach, or hike some local trails. Search the internet for free activities in your area. Look into local entertainment right in your own hometown.

A simple stroll around the block with Mom or Dad could be a favorite childhood memory someday. Place your cellphone in your pocket and set it to silent. Put your phone away and don't answer it! That call is not more important than your child; if you think it is, then it was not the right time to go on that walk. **Be present!**

L...Love

Show your children enough love. Shower them with hugs and kisses. Affection should be in abundance in your home. Let them experience it while they are young, and maybe they will reflect it back to you and others as they get older!

You brought these kids into this world; it is your job to make them feel safe and secure. **Kindness and warm tones should be the music they hear in their homes every day.** Sons and daughters should sense unconditional devotion from both parents. Loving words and smiling eyes show young ones how much you love them.

XOXOXOXOXOXOXOXOXOXOXOXOXO!

M...Manners

Coach your children on manners because they will be judged on them. **Don't let your offspring miss out on opportunities in life because you have not prepared them in social graces.**

Teach your kids to establish eye contact during conversations. Instruct them on how to be a good listener. Show them how to sneeze and cough into their elbow. They need to learn how and when to use the expression, "excuse me" or "pardon me." Remind them to say, "please" and "thank you." Stress table manners like, "Please don't talk with your mouth full," and "Please close your lips while you are chewing." Train them to hold their utensils properly and place their napkins on their laps during meals.

Manners are important!

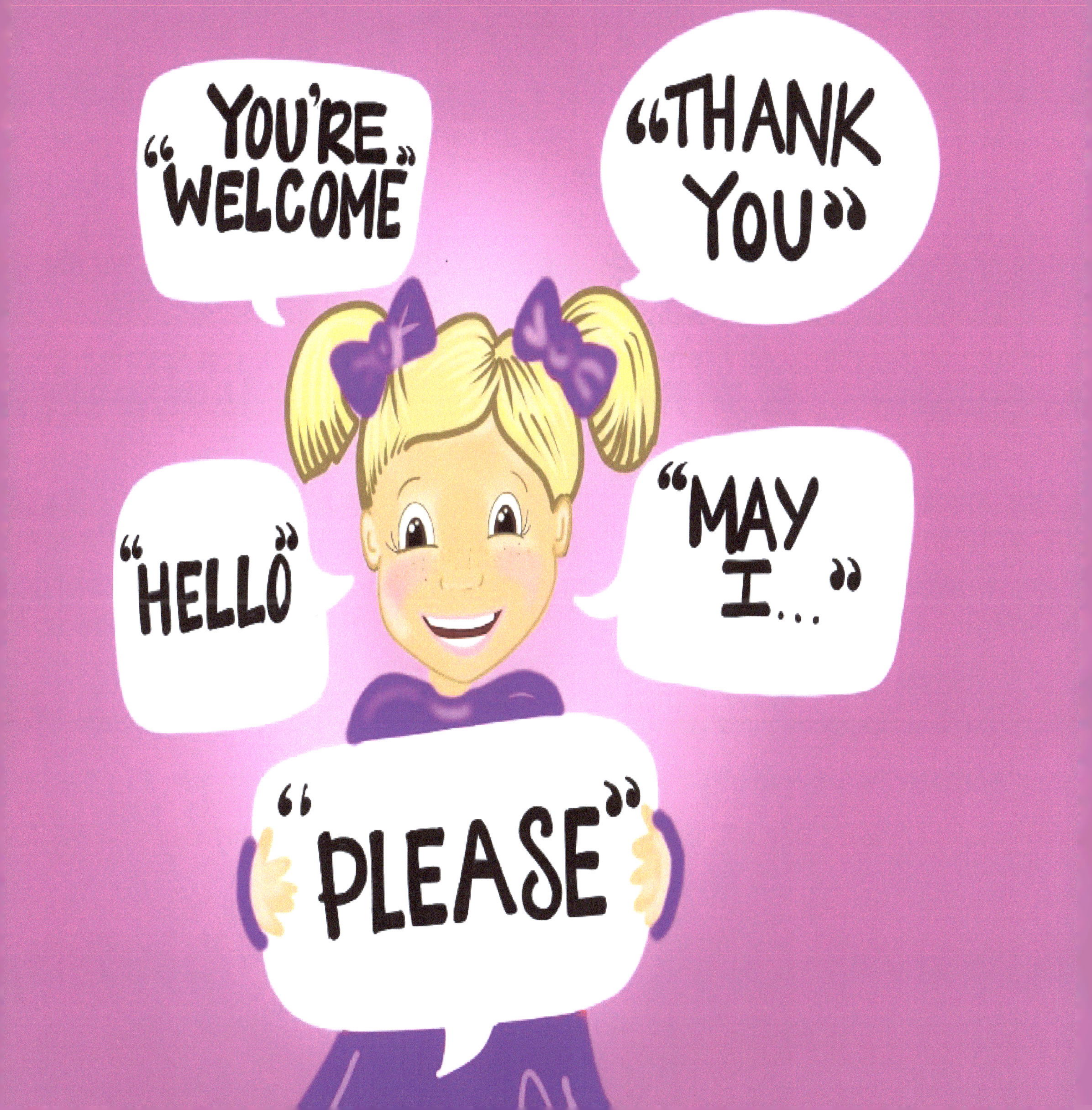
"YOU'RE WELCOME"
"THANK YOU"
"HELLO"
"MAY I..."
"PLEASE"

N...No!

"No" is an important word for children to hear and understand! Parents should use some form of the word "No" often. For example, "No, you can't play video games all day!" This decision won't make your son or daughter happy, but it is the right one. Telling a child "No" is not always easy, but it is necessary. Say "No" and follow through on your resolution.

Permissive parenting leads to children who believe they are in charge. Kids who think they are the boss carry out poor choices based on their wants, not needs. Moms and Dads need to be in control. Little ones with set limits will feel more secure, have better self-regulation, and develop greater self-esteem. Consider it a gift you give to your child. **Childhood is a time of innocence when grown-ups are handling life's responsibilities.**

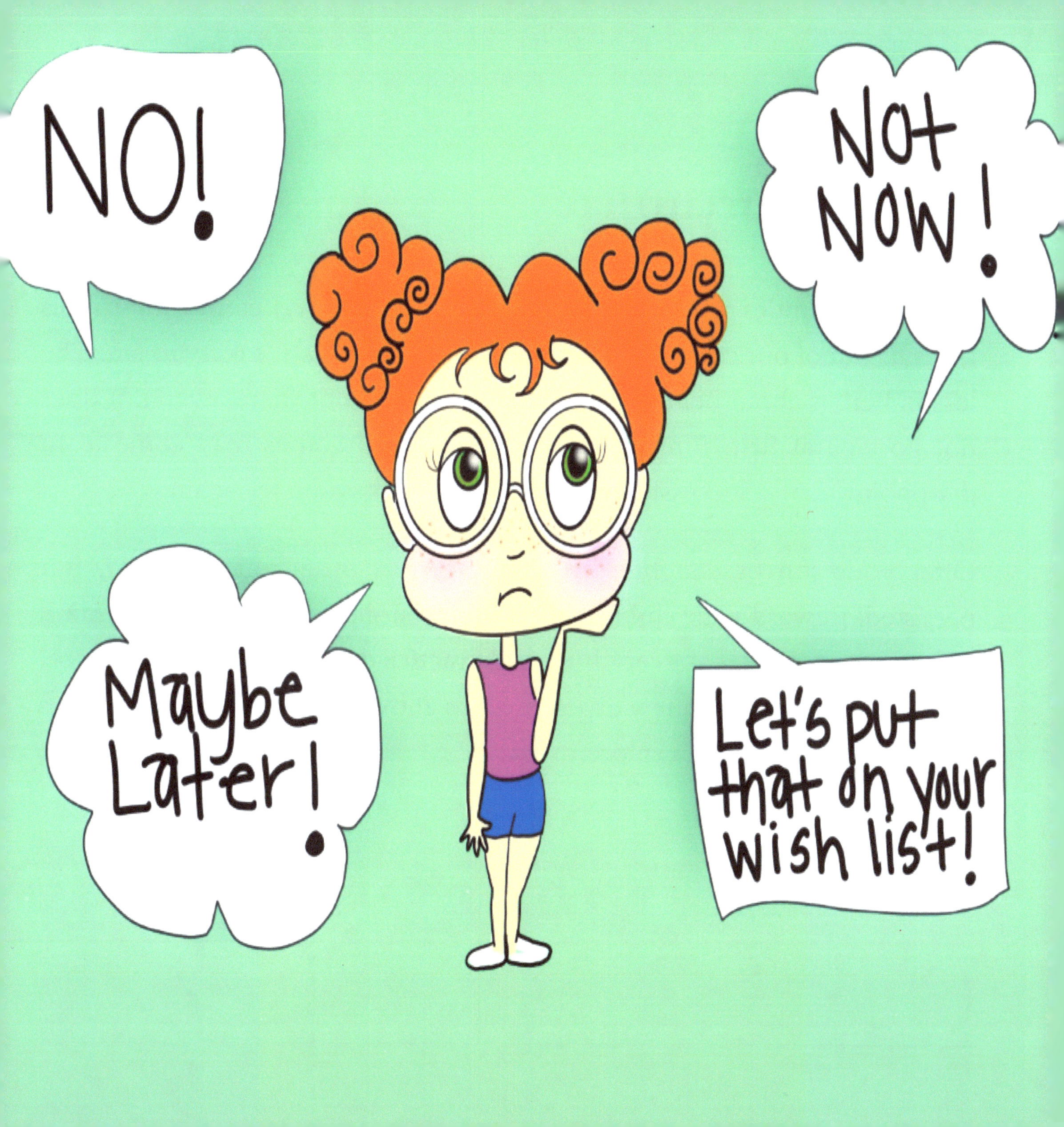
NO!
Not NOW!
Maybe Later!
Let's put that on your wish list!

O...Opportunities

New opportunities provide children with ways to grow. Learning new skills takes us out of our comfort zones. Let your kids know it's okay to fail. The lesson here is about being willing to put yourself out there, even if it does not go well at first. Emphasize that positive outcomes may come from disappointments. Successful people make mistakes and try again.

Offer your son or daughter an example of a time you struggled, but persisted. Reward your child's efforts with a smile, laugh, or hug. **Remind them no one is great at everything and practice can improve performance.** Provide and encourage new experiences to allow your family opportunities to expand, engage, and explore.

P...Parenting

Parenting is about being the grownup in your relationship. You are not your child's friend until later. **You are their parent.** Your role is to make decisions, say "no" when it's appropriate, and be in charge. It's okay for your youngster to be mad at you sometimes; this means you're doing your job! Following rules is a necessary part of life. Kids need these experiences to grow into successful adults.

Children need to learn important lessons from Mom and Dad. Have you taught them about healthy food choices? Are you teaching them kindness through example? Do they know how to stand up for themselves and others if they are being bullied? Take your responsibility seriously and raise quality citizens.

Q...Quiet Time...Shh!

Teach your children how and when it's appropriate to use smaller voices. A restaurant is a good example of when a lowered volume is expected. **Most youngsters need to be taught how to whisper as a skill.** Self-control is necessary! Seriously, practice "Quiet Time" at home when you desire some tranquility. Once your little ones have mastered it, you will enjoy the biggest benefit!

Kids do not have to be hushed constantly. They just have to be capable of self-regulation when it's important, like at school. Your neighbors, schoolteachers, and grandparents will thank you for raising offspring who are a delight to be around. Let's face it: You deserve the peace and quiet, too!

R...Read

Read stories aloud with your children as much as possible, particularly when they are little. **Your child will cherish reading with you because it is time spent close to their parent or grandparent.** Make it a regular part of their bedtime routine.

Hint: Sometimes you have to force youngsters to read before they learn to embrace it.

Visit your local library and take home a large pile of books. Go to a small vendor bookstore and splurge on a couple of favorites. Buy books just like you would spend money on new toys! Try to instill a love of reading early on by making print readily available in your home.

S...Self-Preservation

Parenting is hard, so be sure to carve out some time for yourself! Get some exercise at the gym, meet up with friends, or just grab a twenty-minute walk to clear your head. Schedule a date night with your significant other once a week. **Foster a healthy relationship for your child's sake.**

Don't feel guilty because you need to recharge your battery. You can't be at your best if you are running on empty. Take turns with your partner and give each other a break. If you are a single parent, determine if a grandparent can help, or see if you can barter time with a friend.

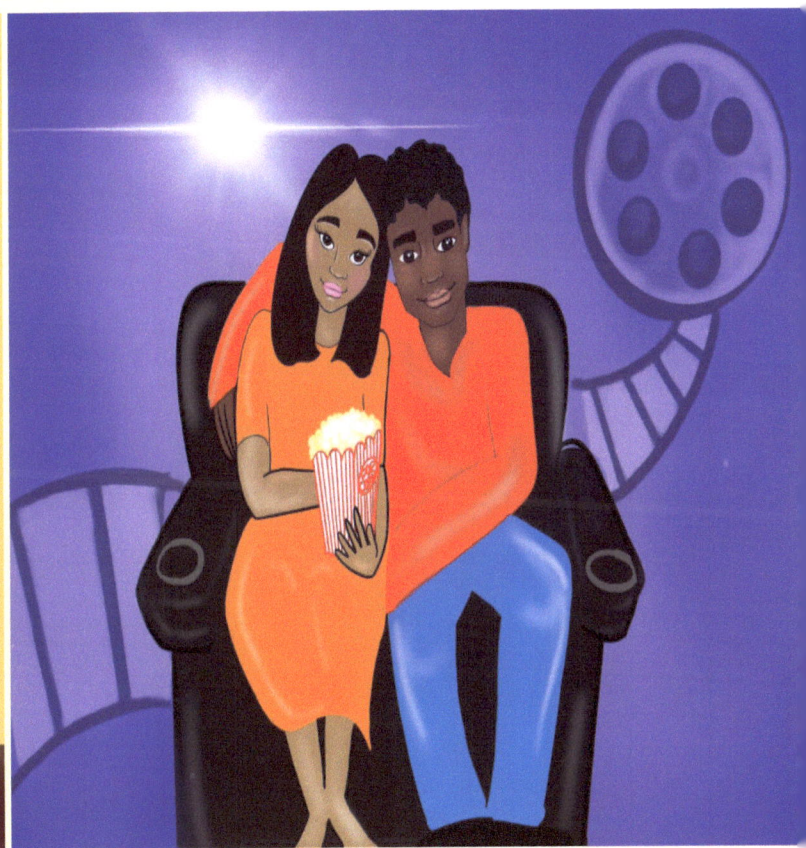

T...Time

Spend time with your children. One of your most important jobs is to make them your top priority! Your parents may offer to help, but be careful not to burden them. Helping should not mean taking over for your responsibilities.

Kids are only little for a short while. It's not fair to expect youngsters to put in a long "workday." During those primary years, seek to create a flex schedule between you and your partner. Working from home a couple of days a week might be the solution. Of course, there are situations where your work obligations are not under your control. Ask yourself the question: Is this the best I can do?

U…Unique

Every child is unique! Each one has a distinct personality and undeveloped talents. Help your little ones explore multiple opportunities to see where their gifts shine. Just because you were great at baseball, dance, or singing doesn't mean that your son or daughter will connect on that same level. Forcing them into your childhood focus may backfire on you. They may lose interest or quit later.

Consider your youngster as an individual. They are not here to be a mini-you or for your bragging rights. Let them lead the way. Encourage them to choose their own interests and help them explore a variety of activities. Just make sure you don't over-schedule!

V...Violence

A steady stream of media violence is not healthy for anyone. Mature audiences and R-rated movies are restricted for a reason. They are not appropriate for younger viewers. **Permitting your kids to be "mature" for your convenience is just bad parenting.** For that matter, there is a drinking age and an age of consent. Don't look for excuses and allow your son or daughter to make poor choices. Step up and say "No" to them. It's okay if they get mad at you...be the parent!

Have you checked to see what your children are watching on TV? Are you setting limits on how much time they are allowed to spend on their devices? Have you checked to see if their video games are appropriate for their age group? It's up to you to stay on top of this and monitor their screens.

W…Waiting Your Turn

Children should be able to remain patient for your attention. **You should practice waiting and taking turns with them.** Do their teachers and others a favor, and show your little ones how to wait! Keep in mind they will have around 20 students in their classroom one day.

Put up one finger or say, "One minute, please!" while you complete your task. Encourage kids to stand by quietly and remain patient. However, be reasonable about your expectations, and be sure to thank them with a hug or a smile.

X…X-tra Love

Love, acceptance, and approval are what most youngsters are looking for from their parents. **Accept them for who they are and not who you want them to be.** This is not always easy! Keep your own hopes and dreams for your babies in check.

Give your kids plenty of love and affection. Speak positive words to them and praise their good choices. Negative messages will stay with children like scars from an injury. Instead, be their number one cheerleader in life. Just be careful not to spoil or coddle them. Help them grow into loving, kind, and caring adults.

Y...Yes!

Absolutely...you can say, "Yes, Yes, Yes," as long as it is coming from the right place. **Do not answer "Yes" because you feel guilty or if you are trying to compensate for working too much!** If that is the case, spend more time (not money!) on your kids.

Plan some weekend experiences to share with your children. You can make up for lost hours during the week by making them your focus on the weekends. Create family memories during these moments. Turn off your cell phones and be present with your little ones!!!

Z...ZZZs

Children need to learn how to fall asleep by themselves! Yup, I said it, and I mean it. Don't let them crawl into your bed with you and don't settle into their beds with them. You may have to listen to a certain amount of whining or crying in the beginning, because they are learning self-soothing skills. Once you set up a consistent pattern, it will get easier. Bedtime is not up for negotiations!

A bedtime routine should provide consistency for your entire family. Start at the same time every evening. Let your son or daughter take a few sips of water, brush their teeth, and go to the bathroom. Reading a book or telling stories at bedtime will help you make it a special ritual with Mom or Dad. All of you will get a better night's rest this way. Most children require ten to twelve hours of sleep every night. Later, get enough ZZZs yourself; you are going to need it!

www.ingramcontent.com/pod-product-compliance
Lightning Source LLC
Chambersburg PA
CBHW041706160426
43209CB00017B/1757